CARTER-STYLE GUITAR SOLOS

ARRANGED BY MARK PHILLPS

ISBN 978-1-4950-0965-5

Hal•Leonard®
CORPORATION

7777 W. BLUEMOUND RD. P.O. BOX 13819 MILWAUKEE, WI 53213

Visit Hal Leonard Online at
www.halleonard.com

All My Loving

Words and Music by
John Lennon and Paul McCartney

Moderately fast

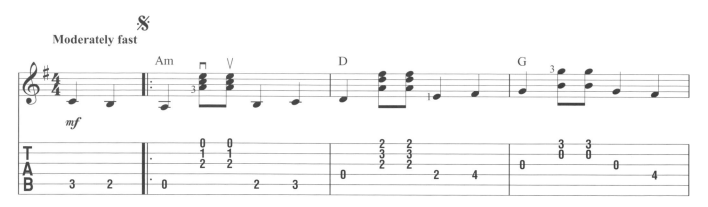

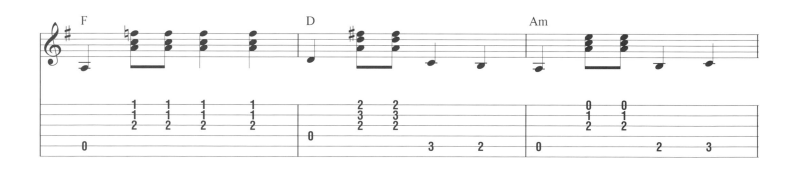

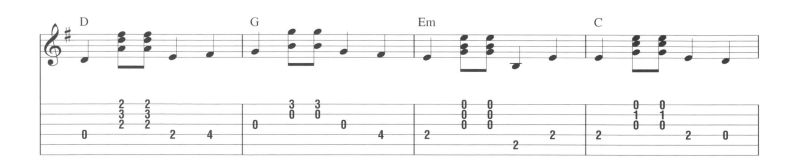

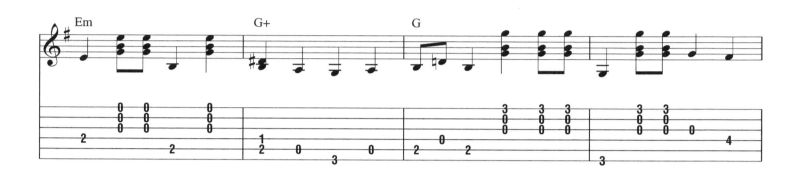

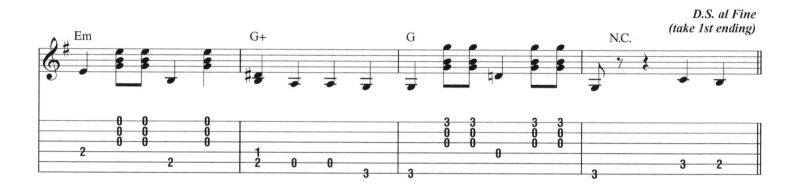

Blowin' in the Wind

Words and Music by
Bob Dylan

Moderately, in 2

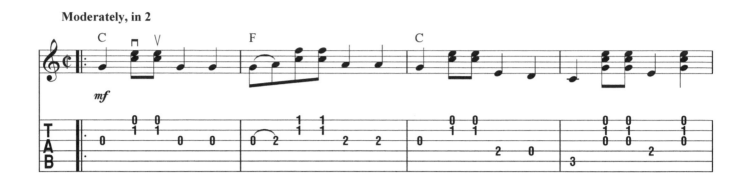

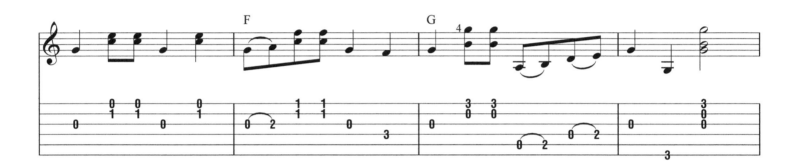

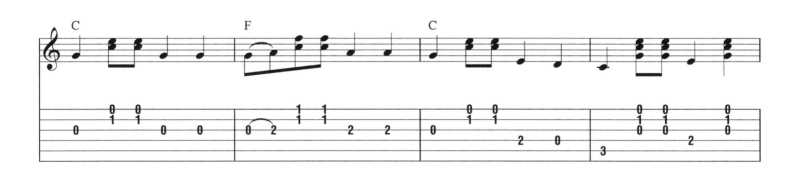

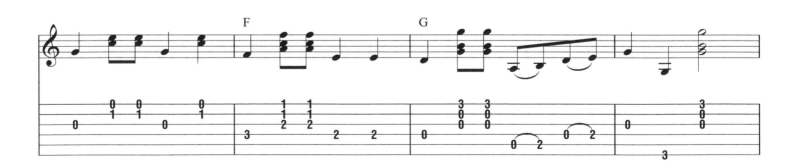

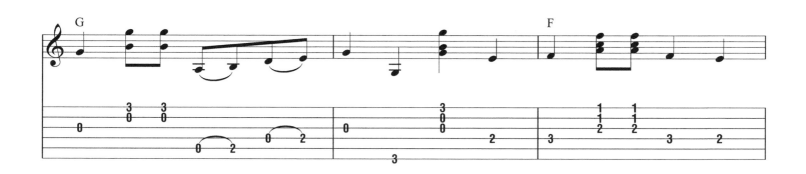

(That's What You Get) For Lovin' Me

Words and Music by
Gordon Lightfoot

Moderately, in 2

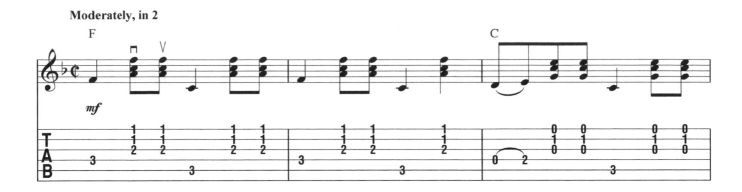

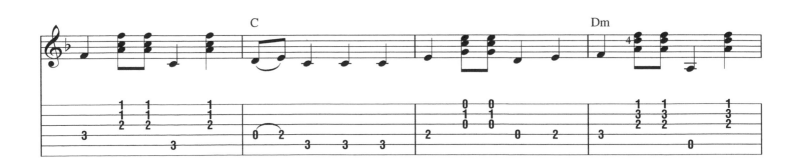

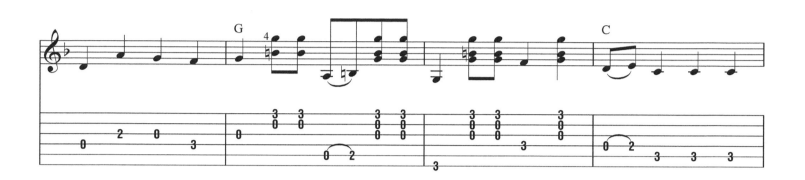

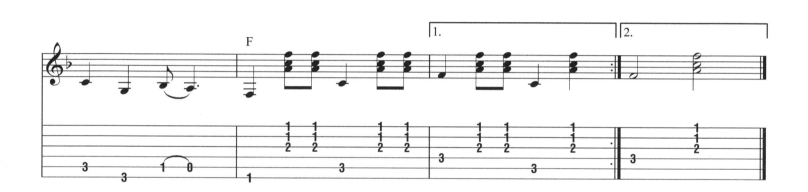

Grandfather's Clock

By Henry Clay Work

Moderately, in 2

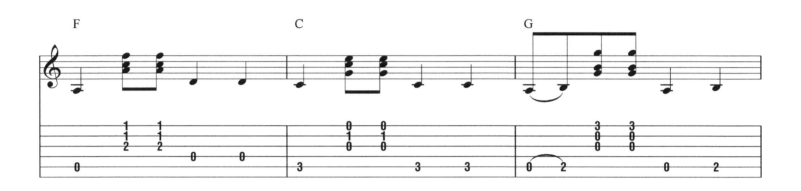

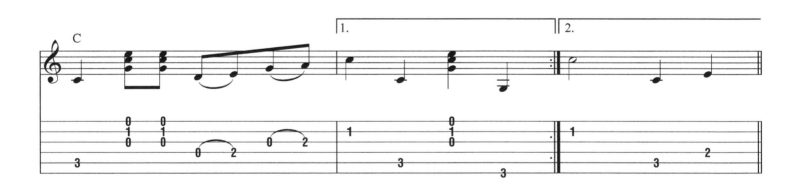

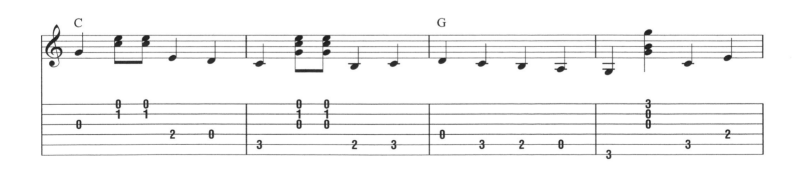

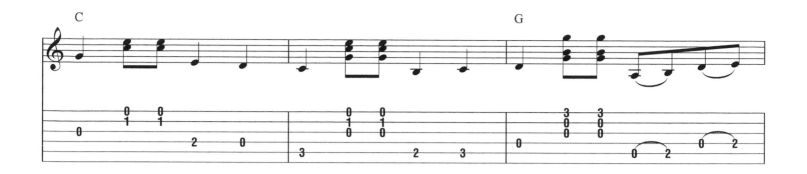

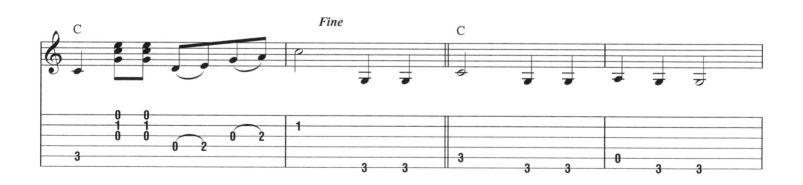

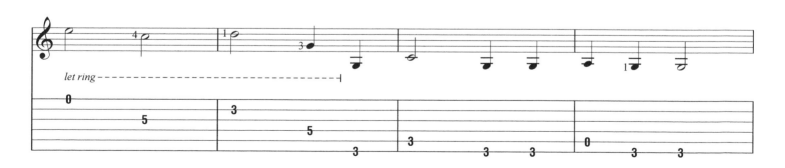

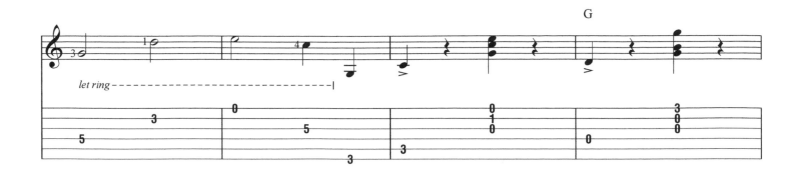

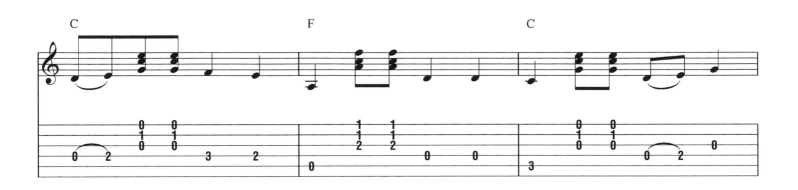

D.S. al Fine
(take repeat)

I Walk the Line

Words and Music by
John R. Cash

Moderately, in 2

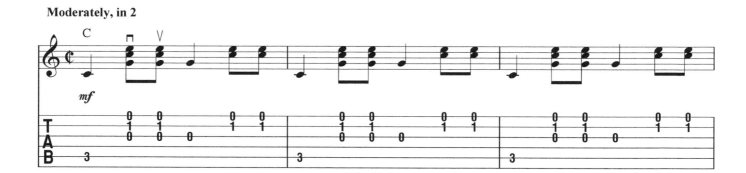

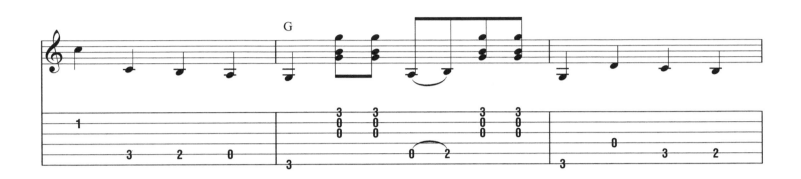

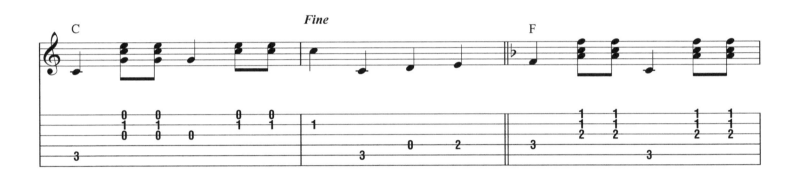

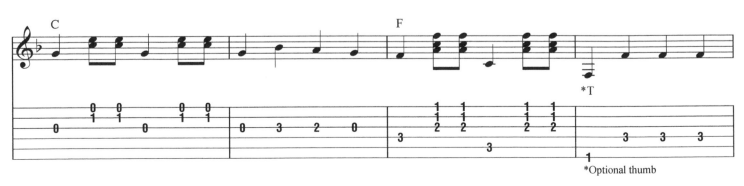

*Optional thumb

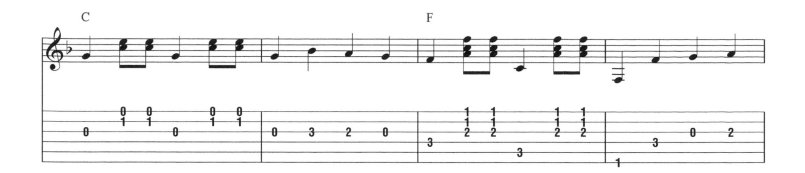

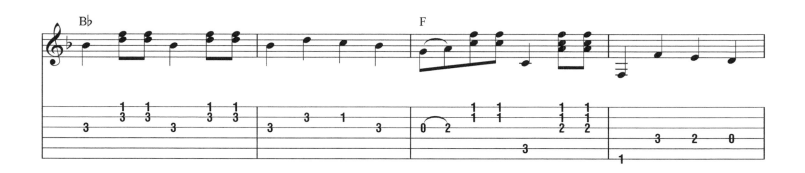

The House Carpenter

Traditional

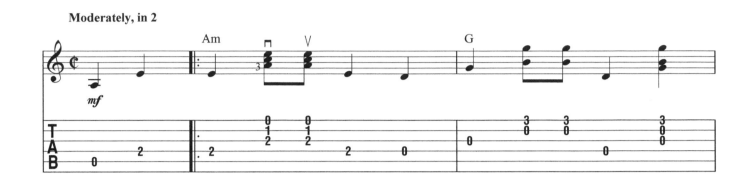

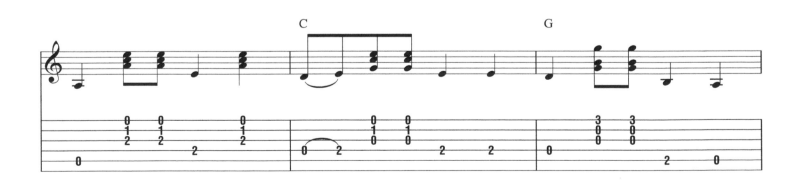

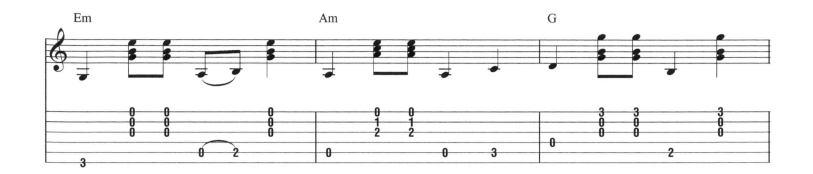

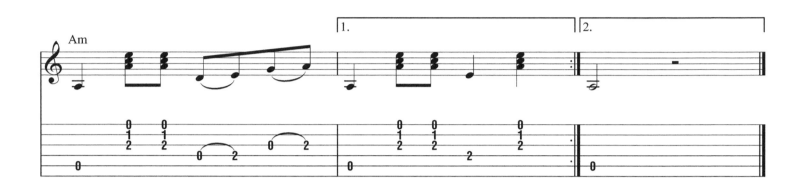

I Ain't Marching Anymore

Words and Music by
Phil Ochs

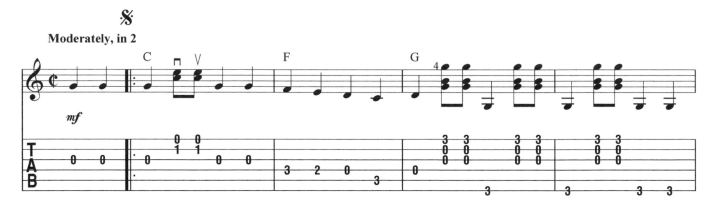

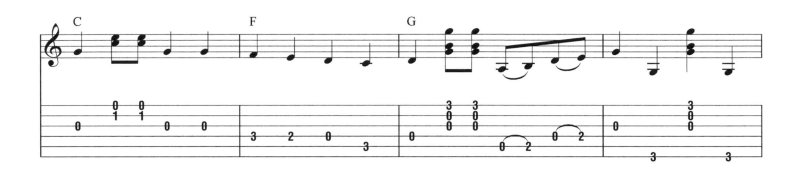

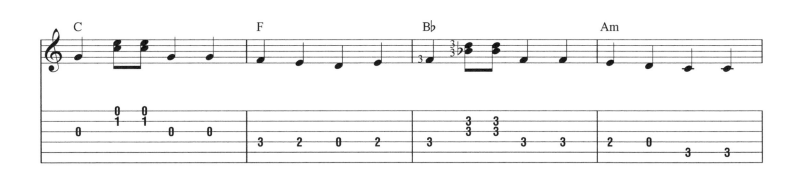

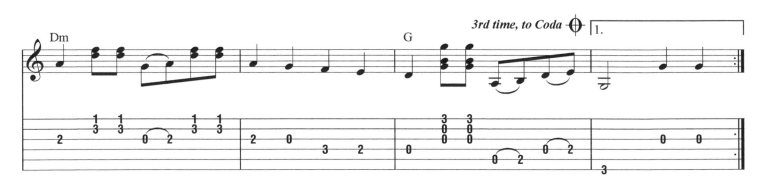

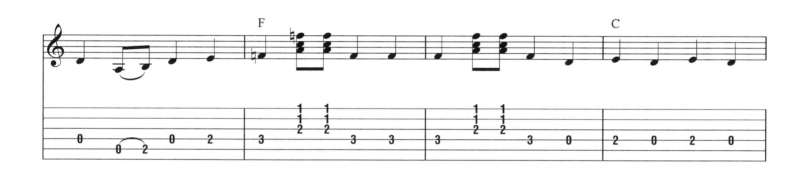

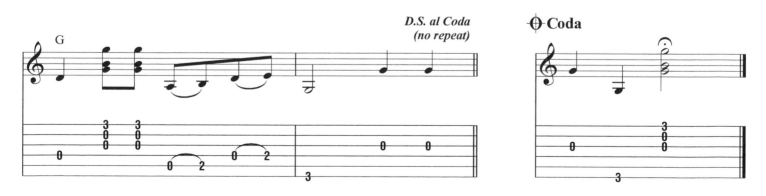

Jesse James

Missouri Folksong

Moderately, in 2

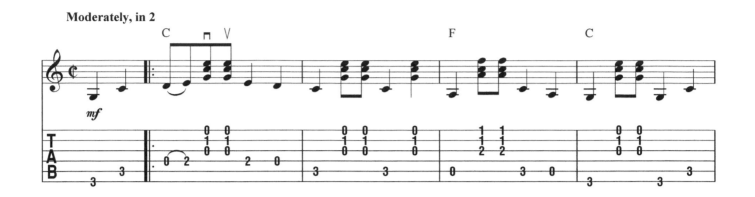

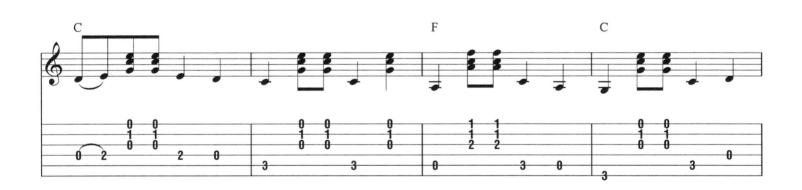

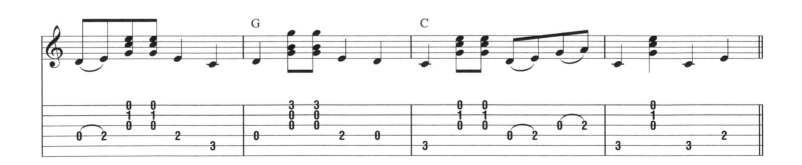

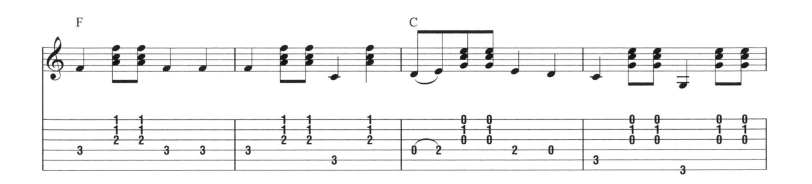

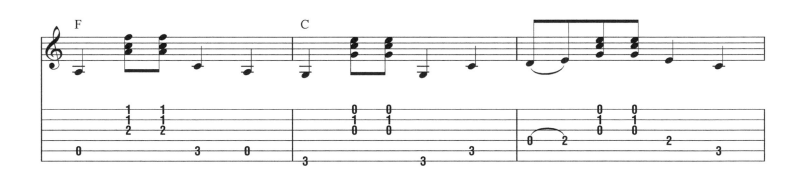

John Hardy

Traditional

Moderately, in 2

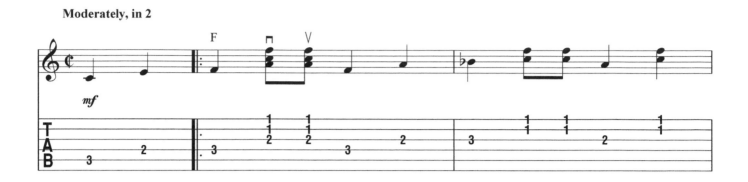

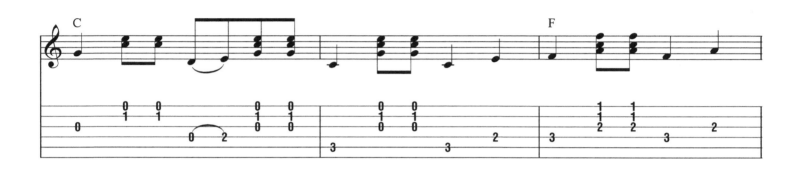

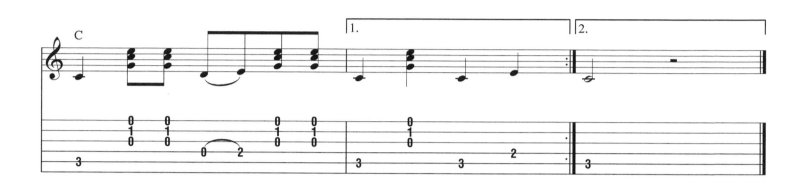

The Last Thing on My Mind

Words and Music by
Tom Paxton

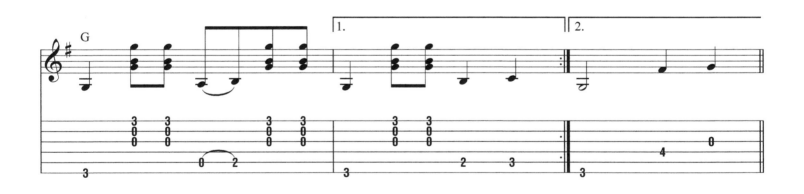

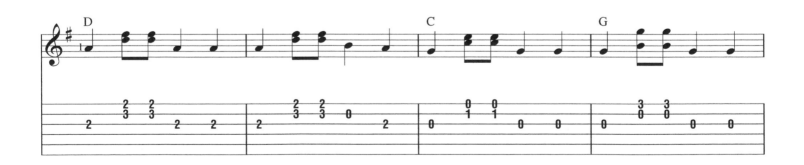

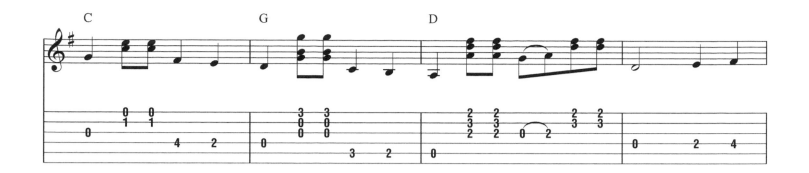

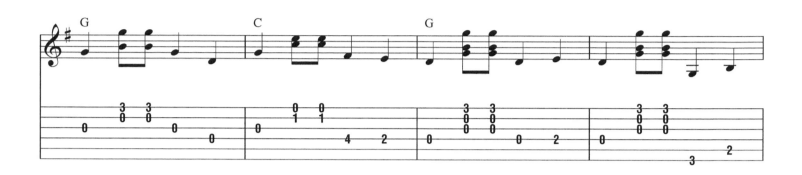

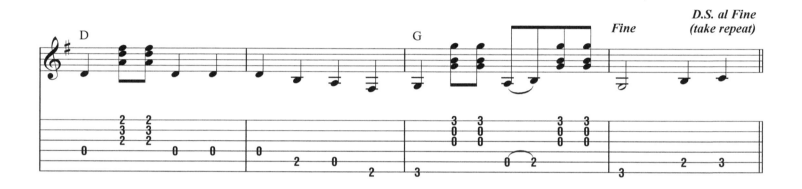

Lookin' Out My Back Door

Words and Music by
John Fogerty

Moderately, in 2

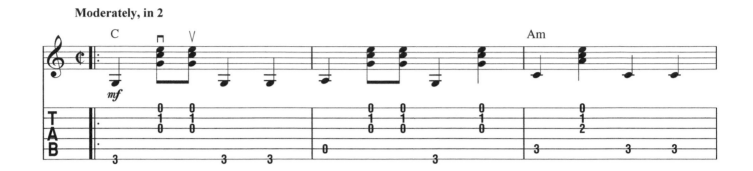

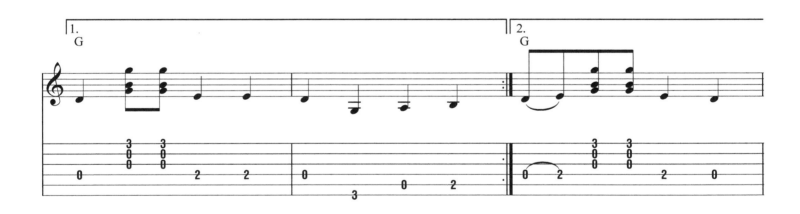

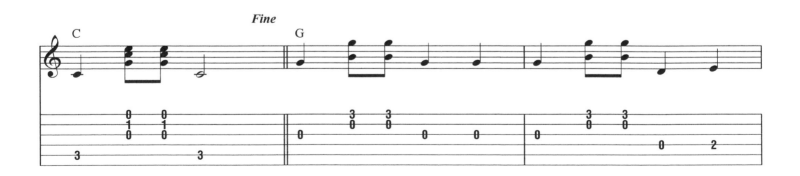

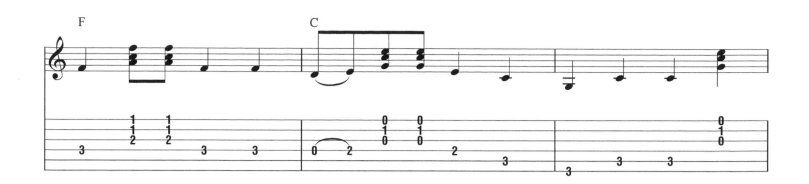

Love Me Do

Words and Music by
John Lennon and Paul McCartney

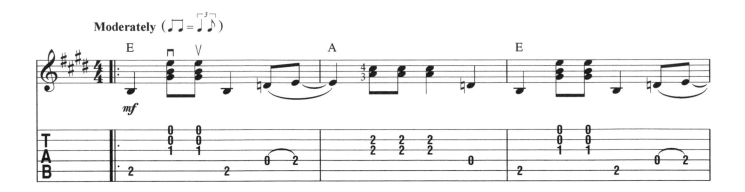

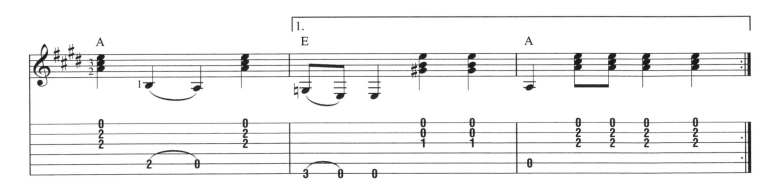

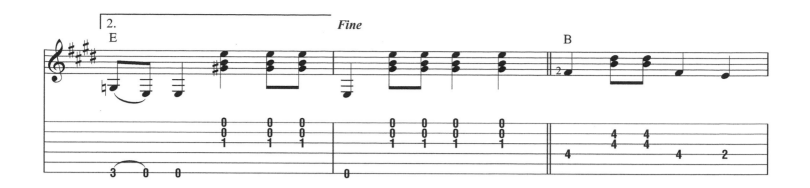

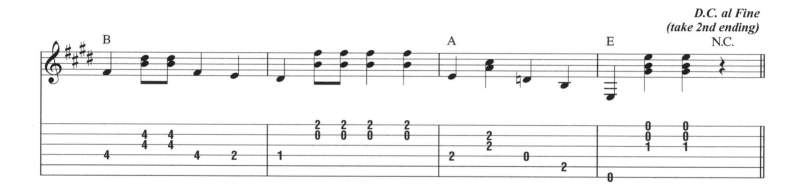

Mr. Tambourine Man

Words and Music by
Bob Dylan

Moderately, in 2

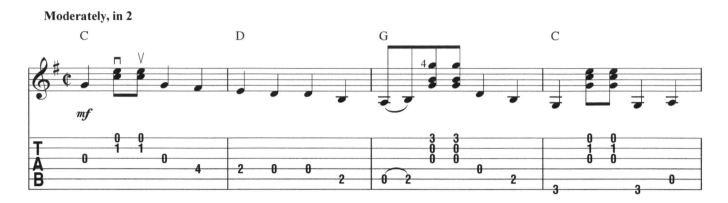

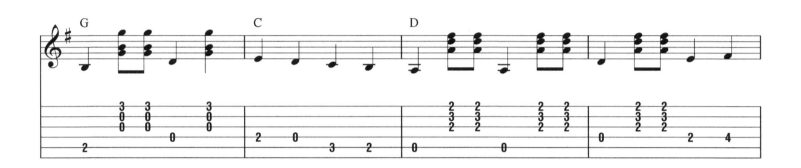

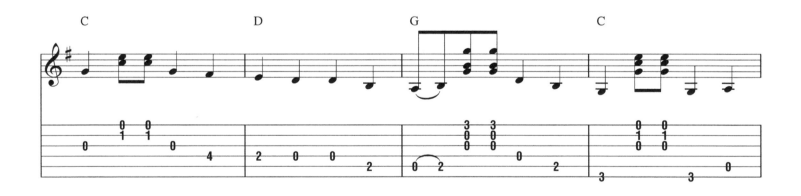

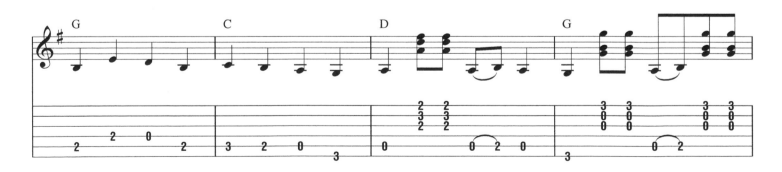

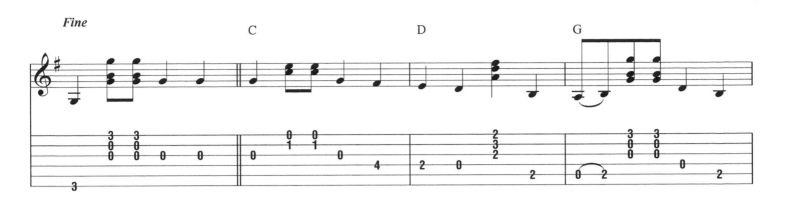

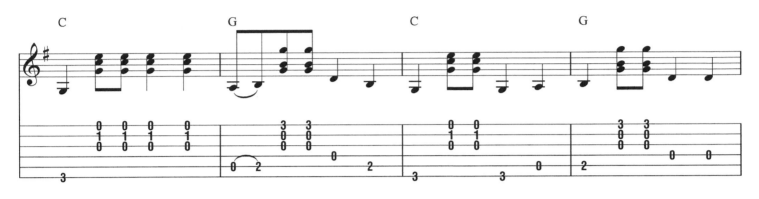

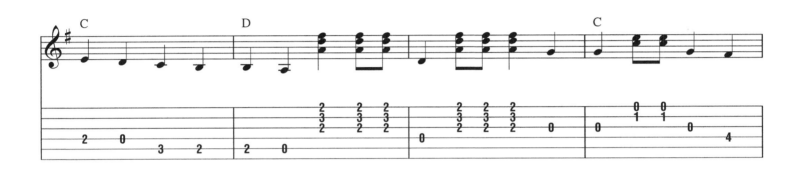

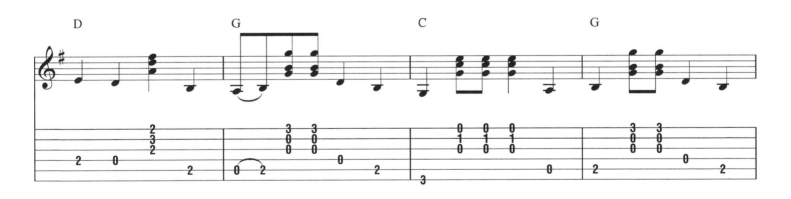

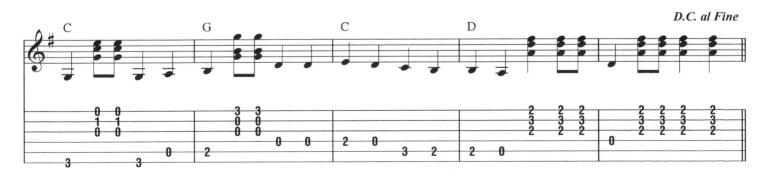

Moon Shadow

Words and Music by
Cat Stevens

Moderately, in 2

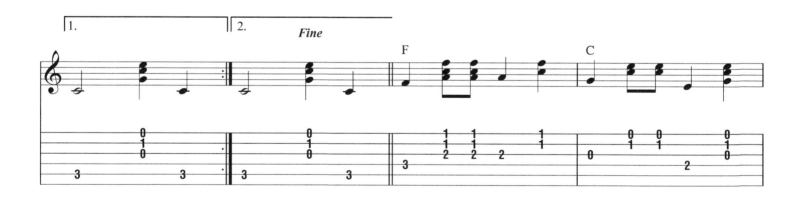

D.S. al Fine
(take repeat)

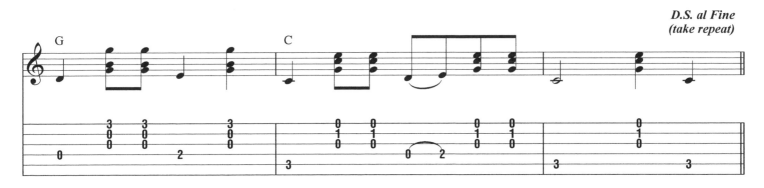

Mother Nature's Son

Words and Music by
John Lennon and Paul McCartney

Moderately, in 2

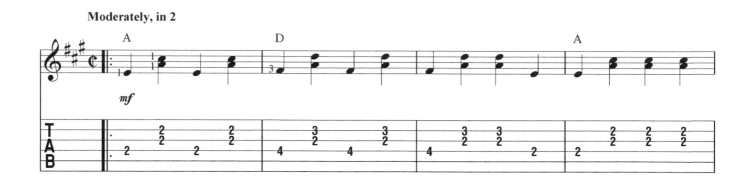

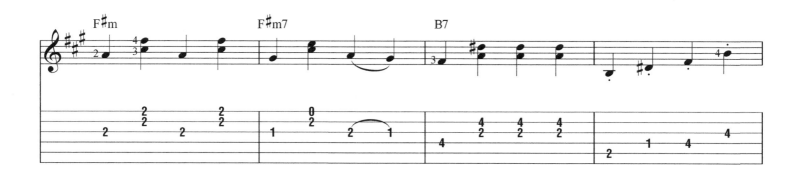

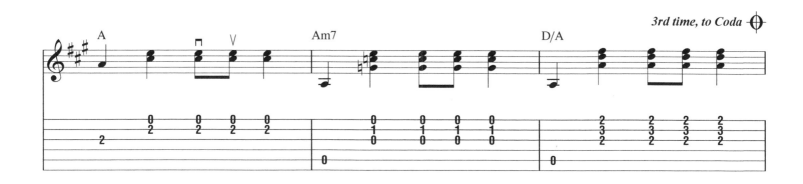

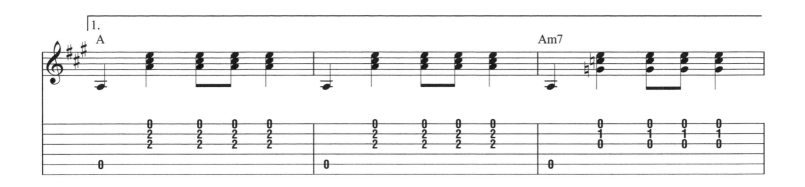

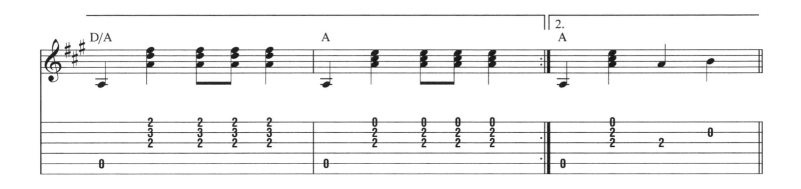

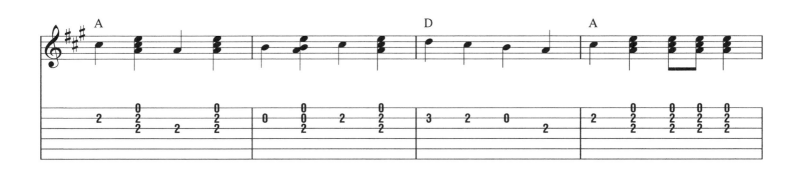

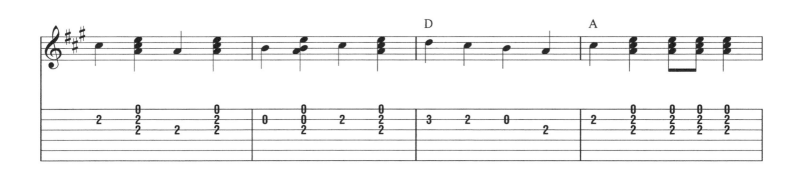

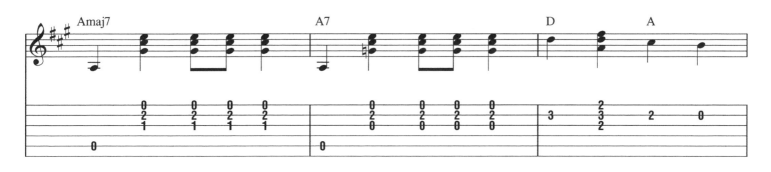

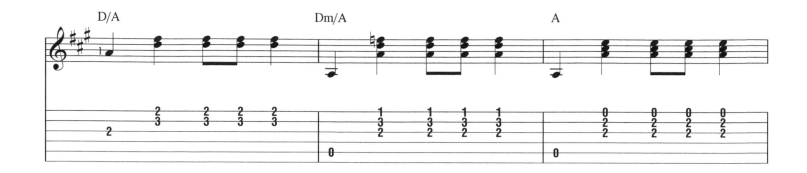

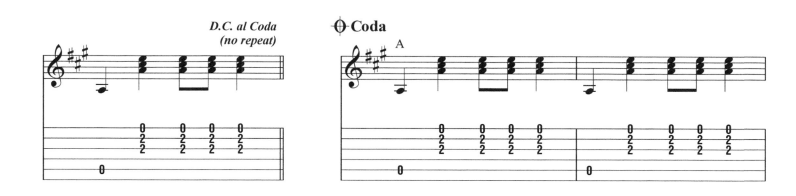

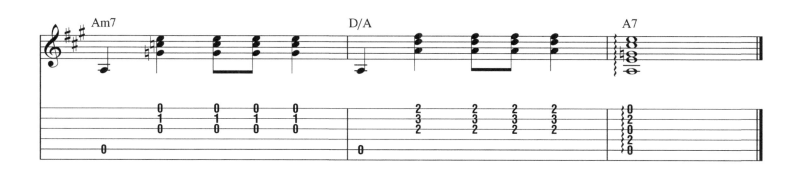

Suzanne

Words and Music by
Leonard Cohen

Slowly, in 2

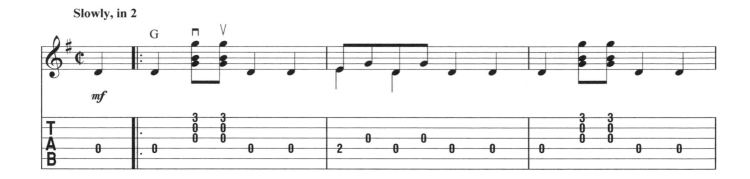

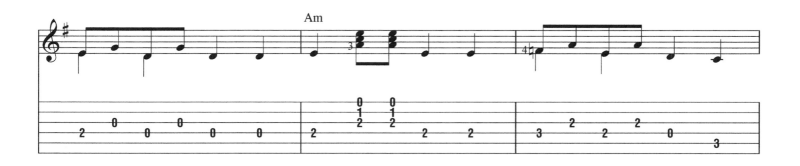

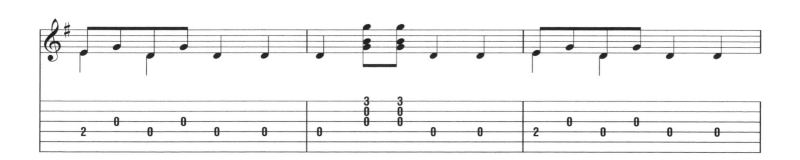

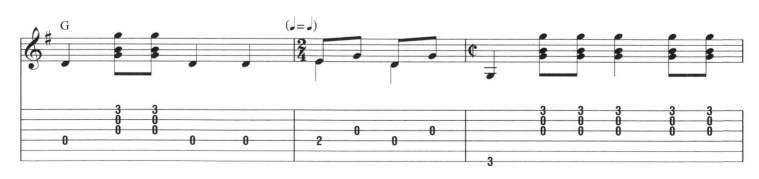

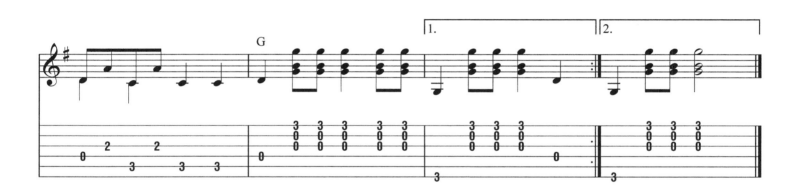

Norwegian Wood
(This Bird Has Flown)

Words and Music by
John Lennon and Paul McCartney

Slowly, in 1

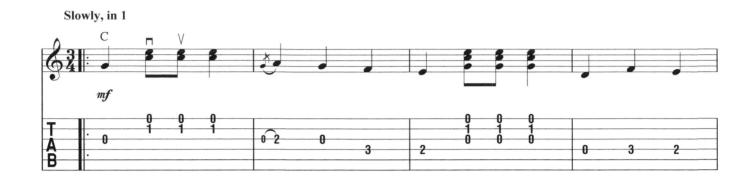

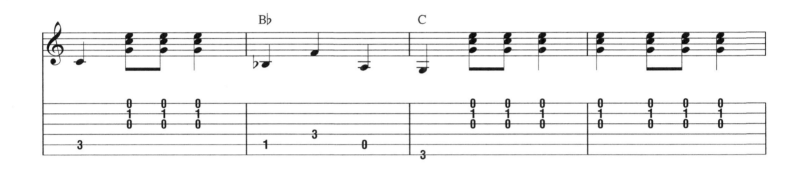

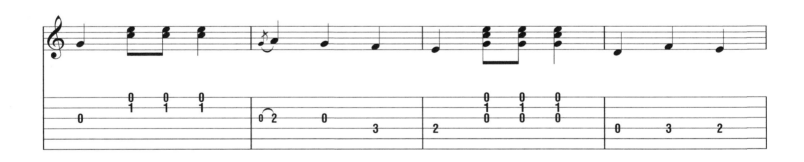

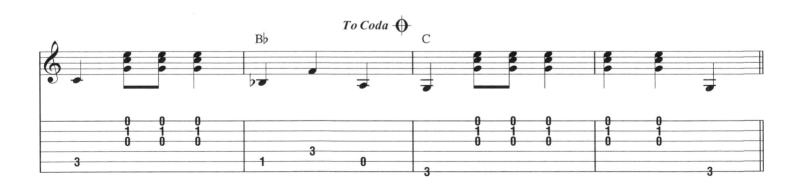

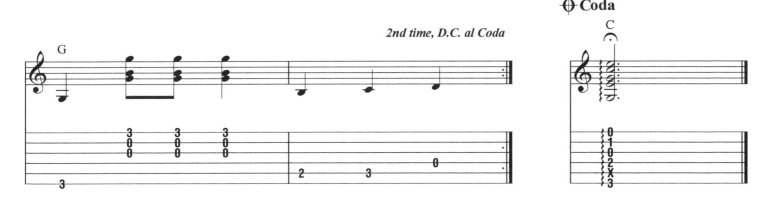

Ring of Fire

Words and Music by
Merle Kilgore and June Carter

Moderately, in 2

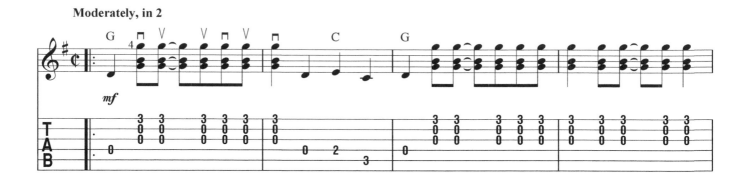

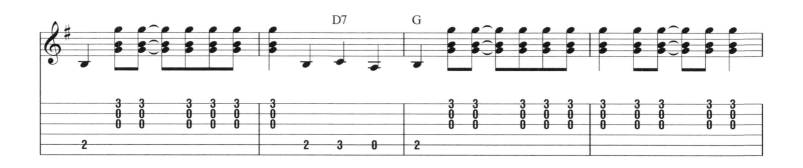

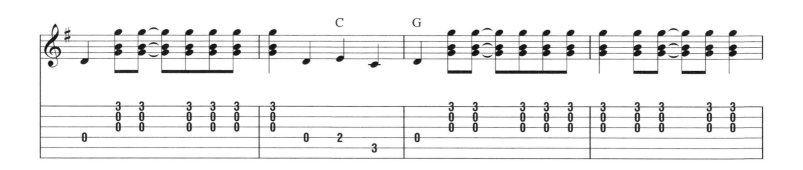

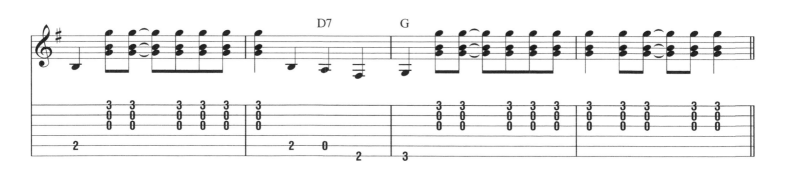

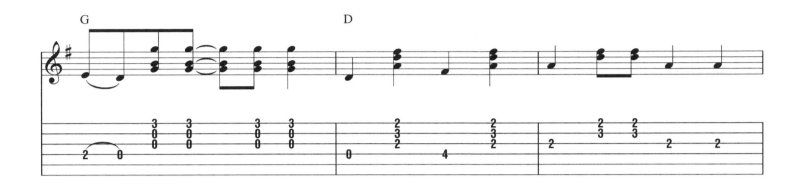

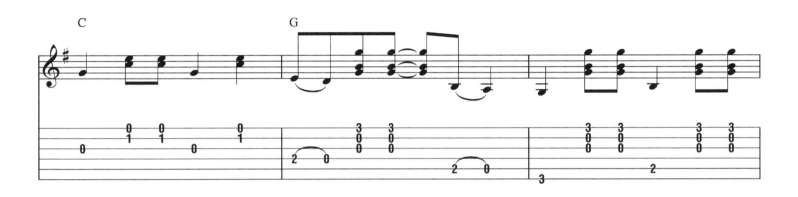

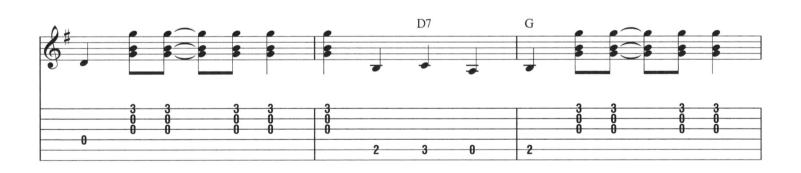

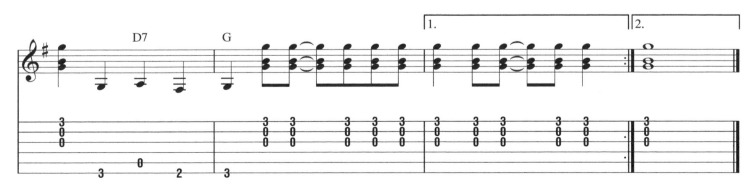

This Land Is Your Land

Words and Music by
Woody Guthrie

Moderately, in 2

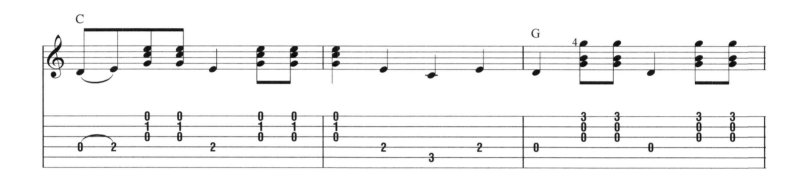

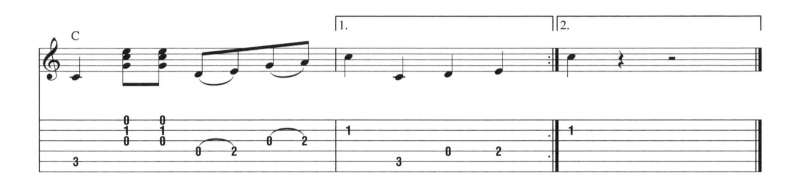

The Universal Soldier

Words and Music by
Buffy Saint-Marie

Moderately, in 2

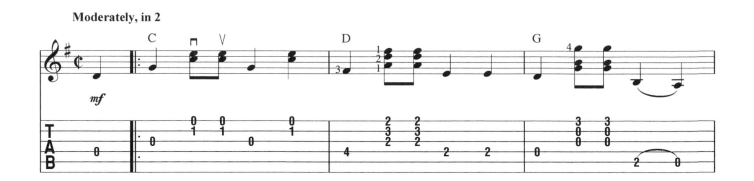

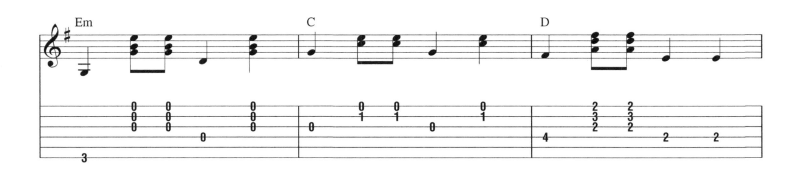

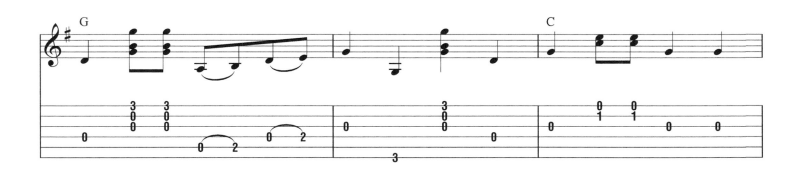

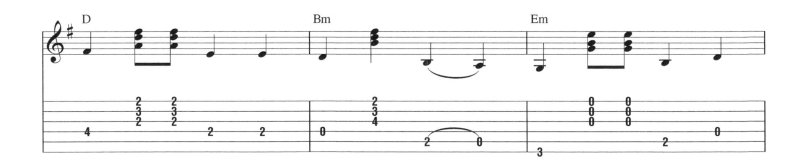

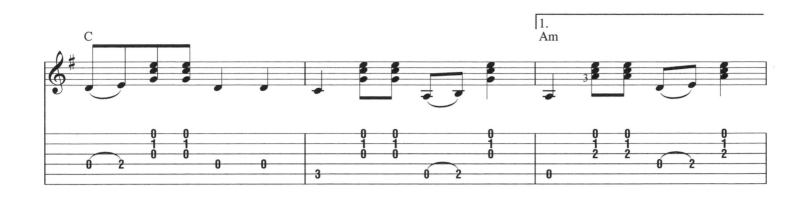

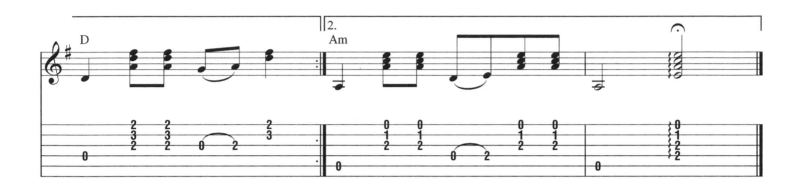

Wayfaring Stranger

Southern American Folk Hymn

Moderately, in 2

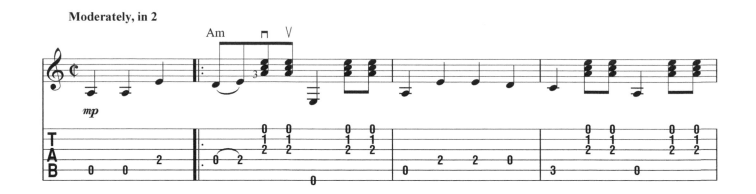

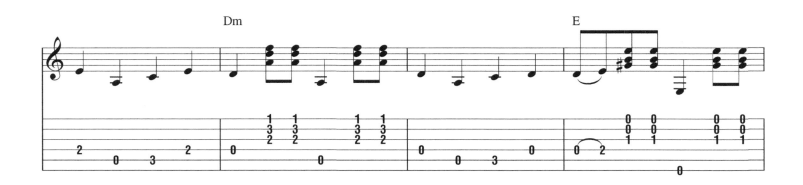

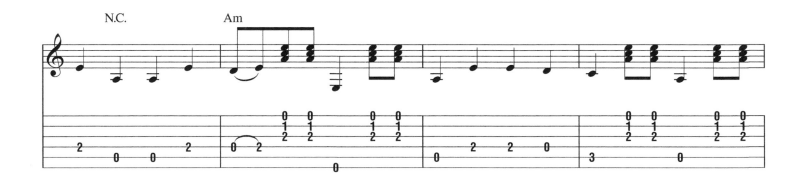

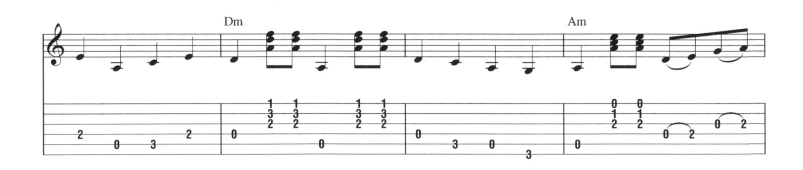

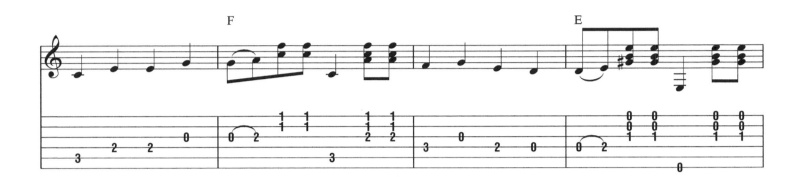

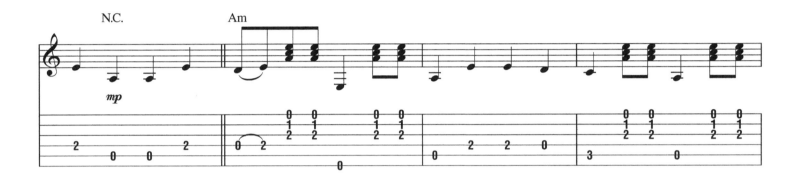

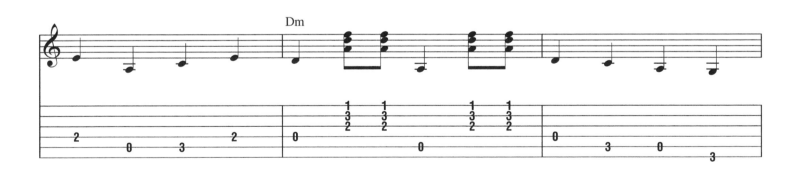

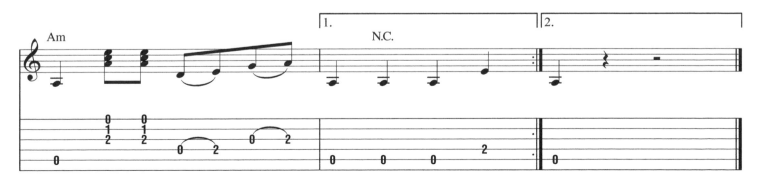

Wildwood Flower

Words and Music by
A.P. Carter

Moderately, in 2

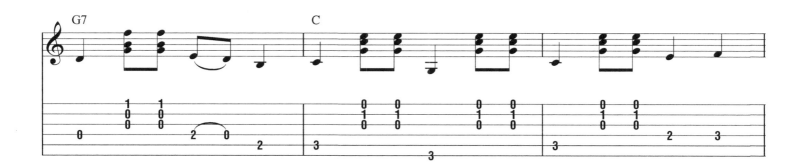

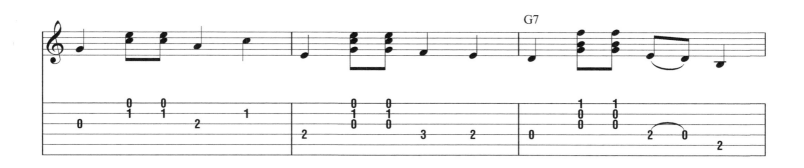

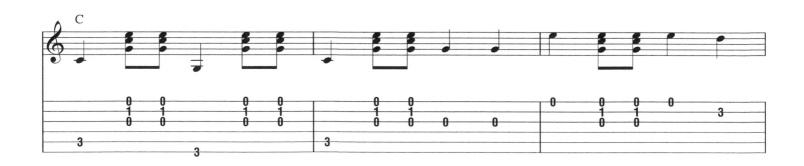

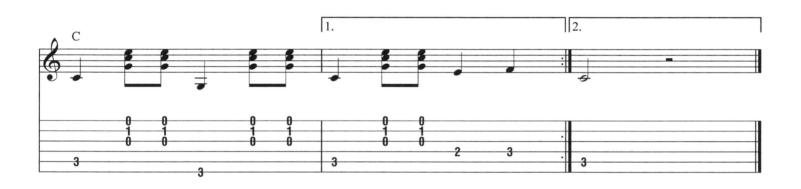

Wooden Heart

Words and Music by
Ben Weisman, Fred Wise,
Kay Twomey and Berthold Kaempfert

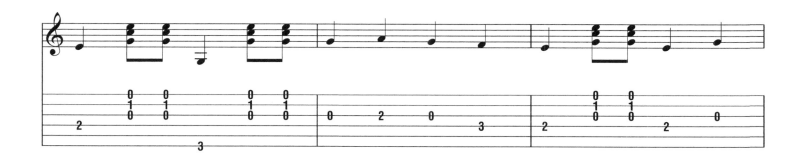

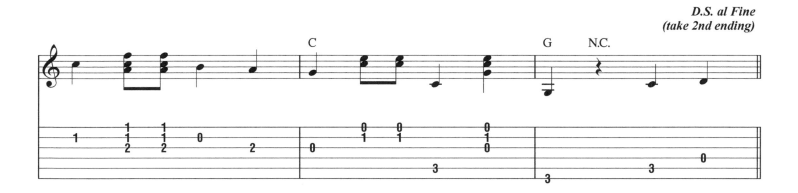

Your Cheatin' Heart

Words and Music by
Hank Williams

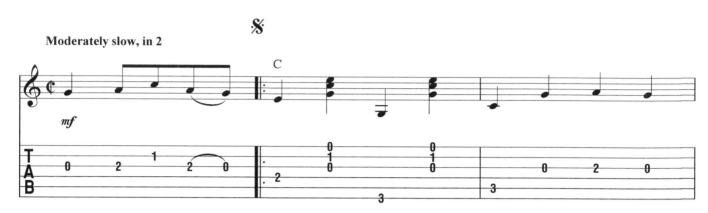

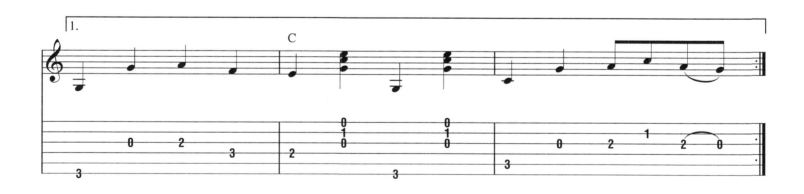

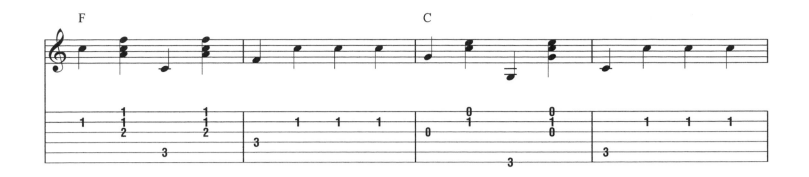

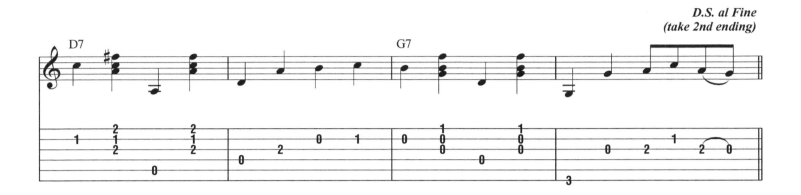

Take Me Home, Country Roads

Words and Music by John Denver,
Bill Danoff and Taffy Nivert

Moderately, in 2

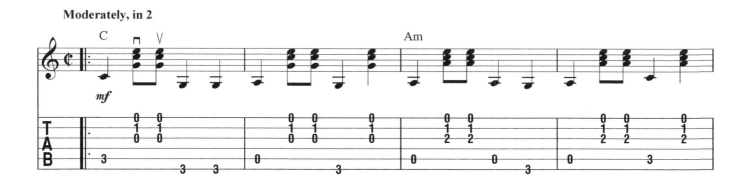

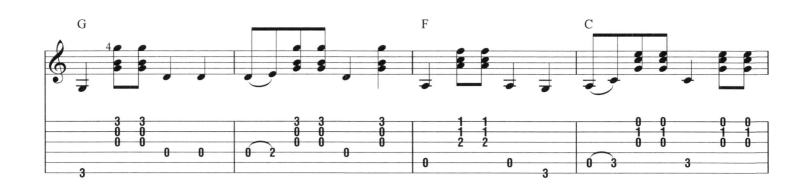

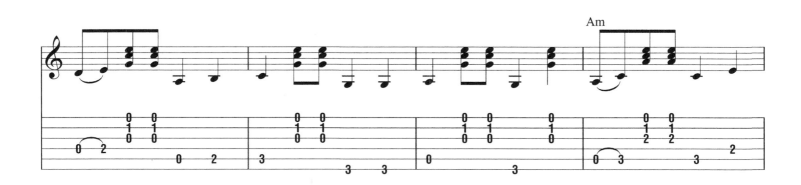

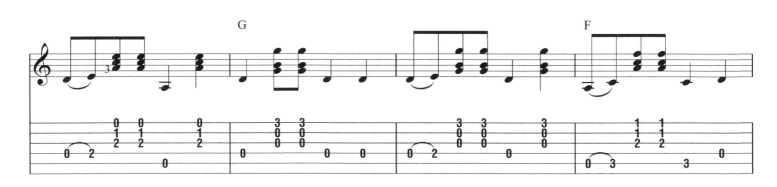

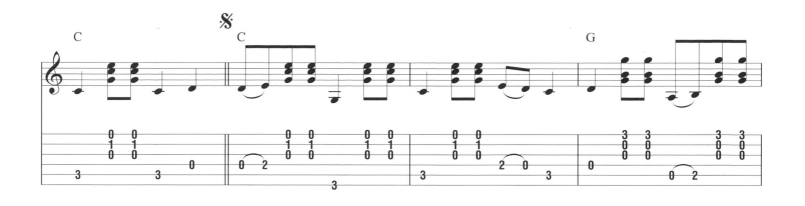

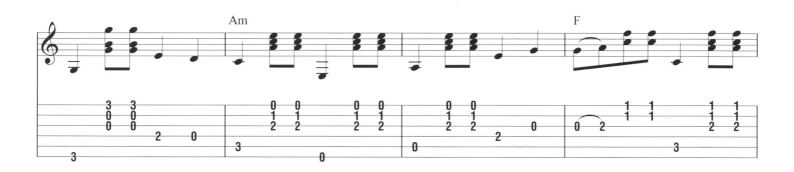

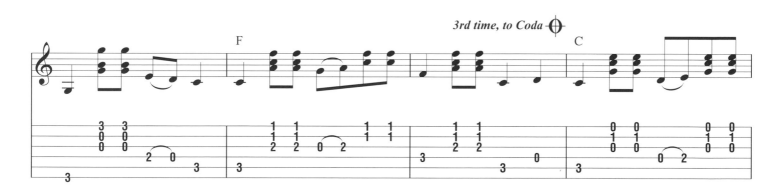

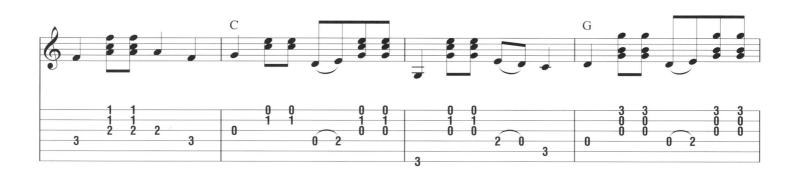

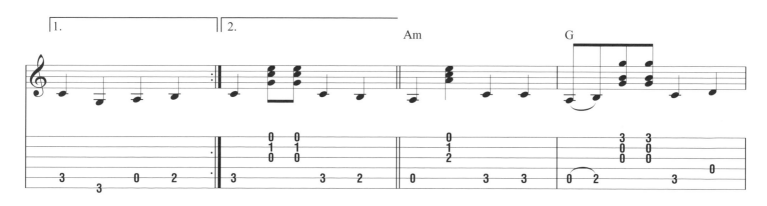

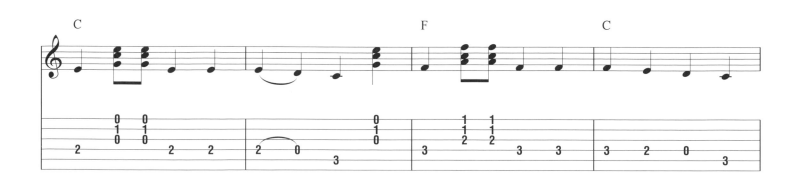

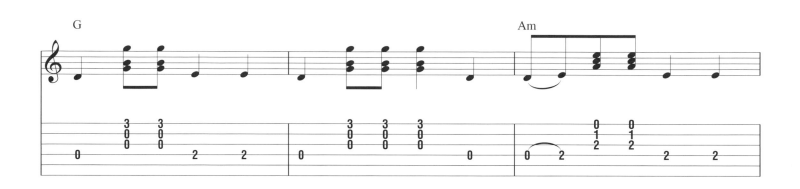

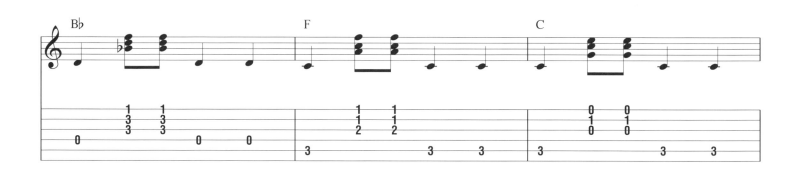

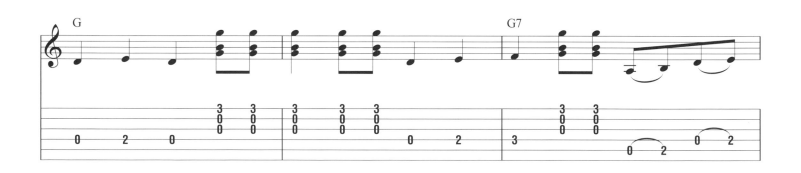

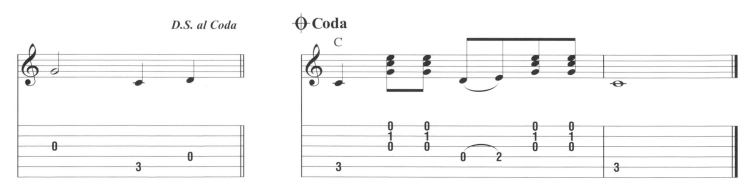